...lage Landmark Churches
page 1

ASHTABULA COUNTY

Congregational Church
Austinburg
page 5

Orwell Presbyterian Church
Orwell
page 6

First Congregational
United Church of Christ
Andover
page 7

TRUMBULL COUNTY

Vienna Methodist Church
Vienna
page 8

Congregational and
Presbyterian Church
Kinsman
page 9

MAHONING COUNTY

St. James Episcopal Church
Boardman
page 10

Poland Presbyterian Church
Poland
page 11

LAKE COUNTY

Kirtland Temple
Kirtland
page 12

South Kirtland
Congregational Church
Kirtland
page 13

United Methodist Church
Painesville
page 14

GEAUGA COUNTY

First Congregational Church
Claridon
page 15

United Methodist Church
East Claridon
page 16

Burton Congregational Church
Burton
page 17

Union Chapel
Newbury
page 18

PORTAGE COUNTY

St. Peter of the Fields
Rootstown
page 19

St. Joseph's Catholic Church
Randolph
page 20

Atwater Congregational Church
Atwater
page 21

First Congregational Church
Freedom
page 22

Church in Aurora
Aurora
page 23

TABLE OF CONTENTS

CUYAHOGA COUNTY

First Baptist Church
Bedford
page 24

Methodist Church
Frostville Museum
page 25

St. Christopher's by the River
Gates Mills
page 26

Independence Presbyterian Church
Independence
page 27

First Universalist Church
North Olmsted
page 28

SUMMIT COUNTY

Bronson Memorial Chapel
Peninsula
page 29

Oakwood Cemetery Chapel
Cuyahoga Falls
page 30

Mother of Sorrows
Catholic Church
Peninsula
page 31

Tallmadge Congregational Church
Tallmadge
page 32

Western Reserve Chapel
Hudson
page 33

Baptist Church of Streetsboro
Hale Farm and Village
page 34

MEDINA COUNTY

St. Mark's Episcopal Church
Wadsworth
page 35

St. Martin of Tours Chapel
Valley City
page 36

Zion Evangelical Lutheran Church
Valley City
page 37

Universalist Church
Westfield Center
page 38

LORAIN COUNTY

Immaculate Conception Church
Grafton
page 39

Christ Church Episcopal
Oberlin
page 40

First Church in Oberlin,
United Church of Christ
Oberlin
page 41

Columbia Baptist Church
Columbia Station
page 42

First United Methodist Church
Wellington
page 43

First Congregational
United Church of Christ
Wellington
page 44

Center for Sacred Landmarks
page 45

Acknowledgements & References
page 46

VILLAGE LANDMARK
CHURCHES

✟

"BUT TRAILING CLOUDS OF GLORY DO WE COME"

WILLIAM WORDSWORTH, *from*
ODE: INTIMATIONS OF IMMORTALITY

Village landmark churches are a unique legacy of the settlement of Ohio's Western Reserve. This legacy represents a *Portrait of Faith* of settlers, the congregations they formed, and the houses of worship they created in villages and countrysides. This *Portrait* is sketched here through images of these early churches and their histories. The 19th century churches presented in the pages that follow are still found today in villages, small towns, and rural areas of northeast Ohio, although some now serve as solitary sentinels in disappearing villages and communities.

The forty churches in this *Portrait of Faith* were selected as exemplary landmark churches because they have significance along one or more of the following dimensions: architecture, history, or their dominant position in their setting. Some have received recognition by inclusion in the National Register of Historic Places. Clearly, there are many more distinctive village landmark churches in northeast Ohio that have great meaning to their communities than are included here, but these forty are a fair representation of the rest. The churches presented here are grouped by counties, and the counties are roughly ordered East to West, in the general chronology of settlement of those who built these houses of worship. The architectural style and date of construction for each church is identified.

This legacy of 19th century village landmark churches and the portrait it forms are fragile. Part of this built sacred heritage no longer exists; it is lost to dereliction and demolition as congregations waned or built new churches. Another part has been

VILLAGE LANDMARK
CHURCHES

enveloped by the relentless urbanization and sprawl of the 20th century. Many of these village churches have been altered, sometimes with limited financial resources, to meet the changing needs of congregations. Additions, handicapped access ramps, synthetic siding, enclosed weather porches, and rehabbing, in some cases, detract from the structure's landmark image.

Setting is an important dimension of landmark churches. They are found as defining points on village greens and the skylines of villages and rural areas, and are a focus for community identity. In this portrait the church images are presented, where possible, in the context of their setting, providing some glimpse of their landmark role in the landscape of community or countryside.

The 20th century, however, was not kind to many of these churches. Some landmark buildings are marred and obscured by modern clutter: new and expanded streets and roads, telephone and power lines, road and business signage, traffic patterns, and visually intervening buildings. In the images presented here an effort has been made to digitally remove this clutter and reflect these churches in their original, more visually serene settings, although this was not always possible.

Some communities have been successful in protecting and, perhaps, enhancing the settings of these landmark structures. Notable examples are Poland Presbyterian Church, Universalist Church of Wakefield Center, St. Christopher's by the River of Gates Mills and the Congregational and Presbyterian Church of Kinsman. The settings of other churches, such as St. Peter of the Fields in Portage County and Zion Lutheran in Medina, have been spared much, but not all, of the marring of modern clutter by their distinctive rural surroundings.

Some village landmark churches have been preserved in their original settings by adaptation to secular uses, such as the Old Baptist Church Community Center of Bedford and Historic Tallmadge Church. Others have been saved by relocation to museum

VILLAGE LANDMARK
CHURCHES

settings, including the Methodist Church of Olmsted, now in the Frostville Museum in the Rocky River Reservation, St. James Meeting House, relocated to Boardman Park, and the Baptist Meeting House in Hale Farm and Village.

Why should we care about these 19th century village landmark churches in northeast Ohio? Many continue to have active congregations that value and preserve the sacred place, although diminished congregations and limited resources are challenging others. These structures also often have heritage significance apart from current congregations. Descendants of early church members may care deeply about these buildings with all their heritage and cultural associations. In villages and rural areas particularly, significance may include a graveyard where parents and other ancestors are buried. Clearly, for these congregations and the descendants of earlier church members, these houses of worship and cemeteries have deep and enduring meaning.

The communities in which these landmark churches stand should care and care deeply. They are an important part of the "identity of place". They dominate and give character to such physical spaces as village greens and rural skylines, and provide a focus for community identity. They connect people to locations because they remain in memory as important landmarks of place. The buildings often anchor a settlement to its history, its values and its sense of community, as well as to its landscape and physical space. Their architectural presence and their steeples and bells orient people in the space of the community and in time. And they remind people, regardless of religion, of a larger context for their lives. They invite them to personal reflection and contemplation of the common good.

Beyond those most immediately and directly affected by their presence, why should we, the rest of us, care about these village landmark churches? Are we made more by their existence and survival, and made less by their loss? Philip Larkin, a 20th century English poet, attempted to put into words the ineffable yet potent meaning of

VILLAGE LANDMARK
CHURCHES

these sacred buildings to those of us not immediately connected to them through proximity, heritage, or denomination:

A serious house on serious earth it is,
In whose blent air all our compulsions meet,
Are recognised, and robed as destinies.
And that much never can be obsolete,
Since someone will forever be surprising
A hunger in himself to be more serious,
And gravitating with it to this ground,
Which, he once heard, was proper to grow wise in,
If only that so many dead lie round.

PHILIP LARKIN,
from *Church Going*

In this poem Larkin reflects on the fragility and fate of these sacred landmarks. He suggests that over time they will have a "shape less recognizable" and "a purpose more obscure," and wonders who will be the last person to seek the church: an architectural historian, an antique hunter, or a tourist to a special holiday service? Or, "will he be my representative"? He seems to be asking who speaks for the rest of us who care and how will our voices be heard?

This portrait of the legacy of village landmark churches in northeast Ohio may be part of the answer to these questions if it succeeds in drawing attention to this heritage and increasing the public's appreciation for it. The reader is also directed to the Center for Sacred Landmarks website (http://urban.csuohio.edu/sacredlandmarks) where a broader set of landmark churches of northeast Ohio is presented.

Congregational Church

2870 State Route 307
Austinburg, Ohio

National Register of Historic Places

The congregation, the oldest in the Western Reserve, was organized with the help of circuit rider Rev. Joseph Badger in 1801. Two women have figured prominently in its history. In 1811 Sybill Austin traveled to Connecticut alone on horseback for 800 miles to recruit a pastor for the new congregation. Later in the century, Betsey Mix Cowles, a prominent Ohio abolitionist and suffragette, contributed greatly to the construction of the current church building. The first service in the new building was Betsey Cowles's funeral service in 1876. The church is located in downtown Austinburg next to a township park.

United Church of Christ

170 East Main Street
Andover, Ohio

as far as the town square. The spire and Tiffany windows were added later in the 19th century, paid for by the sale of the property west of the church. Even without its large west yard, the church has an imposing location on a hillside overlooking the town.

Congregational and Presbyterian Church

6383 Church Street
Kinsman, Ohio

National Register of Historic Places

The congregation, called the First United Congregational and Presbyterian Church, formed in 1831. The Kinsman family donated the site and substantial funds for the construction of the church, one of the oldest extant churches in Trumbull County. The Reverend Joseph Badger, the first missionary to the Western Reserve, preached to the congregation that built the church. The interior has a beautiful coved ceiling, twin cherry stair cases on either side of the narthex and decorated cornices and balcony. The church is located on the highest hill in the town, between two sections of the town cemetery which dates to pioneer days, and near other historic buildings.

St. James Episcopal Church *now*, St. James Meeting House

375 Boardman-Poland Road
Boardman, Ohio
(Inside Boardman Park)

National Register of Historic Places

Settlers to the region of Boardman established the Episcopal Parish of St. James in 1807. The Boardman family donated the land, money and some materials for the church building. The church was consecrated in 1828. It is the oldest public building in Boardman and is believed to be the oldest church in the Western Reserve of the Northwest Territory. In 1971 the Episcopal congregation built another church in a new location, and the empty church was slated for demolition. The Boardman Historical Society spearheaded a campaign to save the church, and in 1972 the church was restored and moved to its present location in Boardman Park. Now called St. James Meeting House, it is used for weddings and special events.

Poland Presbyterian Church

2 Poland Manor
Poland, Ohio

The Poland Presbyterian Church has been located on the village green in Poland since 1802. The present church building is the fourth on the site. The church is beautifully situated in a large park, established by early Ohio founder Turhand Kirtland. The park also contains a pioneer cemetery, containing the graves of several Revolutionary War veterans. The town was named for Polish generals who assisted the Connecticut Army during the Revolutionary War.

9020 Chillicothe Road
Kirtland, Ohio

National Register of Historic Places

largest buildings in Ohio. It has distinctive pews and pulpits; the pews can be shifted to face pulpits at either end of the sanctuary. Community pressure forced the group to abandon the Temple and move westward within months of the building's completion. Today the Temple is part of a building complex relating to LDS history in Kirtland. It is a pilgrimage site for LDS members world wide, and services are held throughout the year.

South Kirtland Congregational Church

9802 Chillicothe Road
Kirtland, Ohio

A group of ten settlers, Congregationalists from Connecticut or Massachusetts and descendents of the original Pilgrims, founded the congregation in 1819. The first church, a log cabin, was built in 1822. A fire destroyed the first building and a severe storm destroyed the second. Church members designed and built the present structure on the same site. The bell in the belfry was made from metals of the Civil War. It is said that local surveyors used the belfry as a fixed point of establishing legal property lines. The church is on a hillside near the center of the township.

United Methodist Church

71 North Park Place
Painesville, Ohio

National Register of Historic Places

The congregation began in 1822, and used several buildings before constructing the present church. The Snyder & Wilhelm architectural firm designed the church following the "Akron Plan," with Sunday school rooms surrounding the sanctuary. The front has two towers, with heights of 97 and 113 feet. The church is adjacent to the town park, the Lake County Court House and other historic public buildings.

First Congregational Church

13942 Mayfield Road
Claridon, Ohio

National Register of Historic Places

The congregation that built the church was established in 1827 and met in members' homes and schools until the church was built. A nearby ancient whitewood tree provided wood for the backs of the pews, the wainscoting, and other trim in the sanctuary. The building may have had a spire at one time. Featured in The Standard Oil Company's 1977 (Ohio) calendar, the church is located in the heart of Claridon Township, next to the Township Hall Administrative Building and a town park.

United Methodist Church

14780 Mayfield Road
East Claridon, Ohio

This church was originally located in Claridon Center which was predominantly Congregationalist, but was moved to its present location in 1867 to be closer to its Methodist congregation. The steeple was added at that time. The church has undergone many renovations, and is now known locally as "The Lighthouse."

Burton Congregational Church

14558 West Park Street
Burton, Ohio

The church was organized in 1866, and in 1890 the building was moved to its current location. It has had several major renovations. The church is beautifully situated on the town square near the town hall, library, fire department, and a large historical park. It forms part of the downtown area of this historic village.

Union Chapel

Route 44, South Newbury
Newbury, Ohio

When the Congregational Church refused to allow James A. Garfield to speak there because they were concernced about the topic of his speech, Newbury citizens built Union Chapel. Unfortunately, the topic of his speech is no longer known. James A. Garfield, later the twentieth President of the United States, dedicated the chapel to free speech sometime between 1856-58. It became a popular venue for scientific lectures and political meetings. The South Newbury Woman's Suffrage Political Club, one of the oldest in the U.S., was organized here and hosted Susan B. Anthony as a speaker. In 1871 nine women cast illegal votes in the building for governor of Ohio, the first female voters in Ohio.

St. Peter of the Fields Catholic Church

3487 Old Forge Road
Rootstown, Ohio

The church is beautifully situated on a small hillside at the bend of a country road. Eighteen German immigrant families built the church, which was originally a mission parish of St. Joseph's in Randolph. The two-room building used one room for services and the other for catechism classes in German. The stained glass windows and stations of the cross were added between 1900 and 1910. In 2005, when the parish decided to build a new church, the old church building was slated for demolition, but was saved by a dedicated group of parishioners. The old building will become a chapel when the new church is constructed.

St. Joseph's Catholic Church

2643 Waterloo Road
Randolph, Ohio

The parish was formed in 1829 by German Catholic farmers who settled in southern Portage County. A cemetery and a grotto form part of the extensive grounds. The ornate interior has beautiful stained glass windows and statuary. The church is located on a country road.

Atwater Congregational Church

1237 State Route 183
Atwater, Ohio

National Register of Historic Places

The congregation that built the church was formed in 1818. The church dominates the public green which also contains a cemetery and a town hall. Architecturally, the church resembles many New England churches of the colonial and federal periods. However, the pointed windows show the influence of Gothic style, which was beginning to have a revival at the time the church was built.

First Congregational Church

Public Green on OH 88
Freedom, Ohio

National Register of Historic Places

The congregation that built the church consisted mainly of settlers from New England who were descendants of the Pilgrims. They organized the church in 1828 and met in a school house until the church was completed in 1845. A local contractor, Ralph W. Shepard, won a competition to design and build the church. Local legend tells that one dedicated early parishioner rode an ox through the woods to get to the church as the roads were not yet opened, and ruined her dresses as they got torn on the bushes. The bell in the steeple was an important part of village life; on the day of Abraham Lincoln's funeral, the bell ringer tolled the bell for two hours.

1872 | CARPENTER GOTHIC | PORTAGE COUNTY

Church in Aurora

146 South Chillicothe Road
Aurora, Ohio

The Aurora Center Historic District is listed on the National Register of Historic Places.

The original church was Congregational, formed in 1809 shortly after Aurora was founded. In 1913 the Disciples Church joined the Congregationalists and in 1933 the combined church was renamed the Church in Aurora. It now has members from over 40 different Christian denominations. The church is located on a hillside with a large sloping lawn in front. It sits next to the Town Hall at the main intersection of town.

First Baptist Church, *now* Old Baptist Church Community Building

750 Broadway Avenue
Bedford, Ohio

National Register of Historic Places

Prominent architect Jacob Snyder designed the church in the popular "Akron plan," a style which originated in Akron, Ohio and then spread throughout the United States. Design elements include a sloped sanctuary with curved pews radiating from the pulpit, and Sunday School classrooms clustered adjacent to the main sanctuary. The church houses a 1914 Moeller Pipe Organ. Located in downtown Bedford, the church stands beside several historic buildings framing a city park called "Bedford Commons," and is now used for community events.

Methodist Church
now part of the
Frostville Museum
Rocky River Reservation

Olmsted Historical Society
Frostville Museum

Located off Cedar Point Road west of Valley Parkway in the Rocky River Reservation

The origins of this Olmsted church are in doubt. Originally thought to be the Union House of Worship, recent research suggests that it may have been built by Methodists in Olmsted in 1847 and sold to the Congregationalists in 1871. The building has undergone several major renovations, and it is no longer certain what the original building looked like. The Congregational Church closed in the 1970s, and the church subsequently changed ownership twice. It suffered deterioration. The Olmsted Historical Society acquired the building in June, 2005, and moved it from its original location in historic Olmsted to the Frostville Museum, a restored 1800s community. The cupola of this church is pictured below.

St. Christopher's by the River

17601 Old Mill Road
Gates Mills, Ohio

National Register of Historic Places

This church was built by a Methodist congregation with donations from the town founder, Halsey Gates. In 1906 the Episcopal Church began to hold vesper services there. In 1926 a canvass of the neighborhood revealed the community wished the church to become Episcopalian, and it was established as an Episcopal mission church that same year. The name changed to St. Christopher's by the River. It is located between a bank of the Chagrin River and the main road of the village, near other historic buildings.

Independence Presbyterian Church

6624 Public Square
Independence, Ohio

National Register of Historic Places

The Missionary Association of Connecticut formed the original congregation in 1837 with seven members. The meetings were first held in a log school house and later in the town hall. In 1862 the congregation became Presbyterian. The building is constructed of local sandstone, and is located on the west side of the town square in the historic downtown district. Today, the old sandstone edifice remains, but has been joined by a modern, larger church building. The two buildings are linked by a well-landscaped courtyard.

First Universalist Church

5050 Porter Road
North Olmsted, Ohio

National Register of Historic Places

Settlers to the area founded the Universalist congregation in 1834. The building is the oldest church in North Olmsted and one of the first Universalist churches in Ohio. The belfry was used as a station in the Underground Railway, hiding escaped slaves before the Civil War. The architecture is typical of the time, based on small Greek temples capped with a tower and adorned with Gothic elements, such as the window over the front door of the church. This building, originally located in historic Olmsted, was moved to its current location in 1963.

Bronson Memorial Church *now*, Bronson Memorial Church Museum

1712 Main Street
Peninsula, Ohio

Part of the Peninsula Village Historic District, listed on the National Register of Historic Places.

This Episcopal church, originally called Bethel Church, was built in 1835 by Hermon Bronson who wanted to "introduce moral and religious tactics among the vicious and unlawful practices of the canal boatmen." (William Perrin's *History of Summit County*, 1881). The church was remodeled in Gothic Revival style in 1889 and renamed Bronson Memorial Church, after the donor of funds for the remodeling. Church membership waned in the 20th century, and in 1965 the Episcopal Diocese donated the building to the Ohio Historical Society. The Society now maintains the building, which is used for weddings and other special events.

Oakwood Cemetery Chapel

2420 Oakwood Drive
Cuyahoga Falls, Ohio

National Register of Historic Places

The Ladies Cemetery Association built this non-denominational chapel for use by families and friends of those buried in Oakwood Cemetery. Of special significance are the twelve stained glass windows sponsored by founding families and organizations of the city. The Chapel was used regularly for services until the mid 1930s and is still used for meetings of the Ladies Cemetery Association. The chapel is located on the cemetery grounds.

Mother of Sorrows Catholic Church

6034 Locust Street
Peninsula, Ohio

Located in the Peninsula Historic District listed on the National Register of Historic Places.

This church was built for descendants of Irish Catholics who came to Ohio in the 1820s to build the Ohio and Erie canals. Originally called by its Latin name, "Mater Dolorosa," it was very plain and did not have a finished interior until 1887. In the early twentieth century, Catholics from Eastern Europe arrived in the community to work in the paper mills, and the congregation grew rapidly. In 1935, the church was expanded by cutting the building in two, moving the altar section back, and constructing a new middle section. The church was completely renovated for its centennial celebration in 1982.

Tallmadge Congregational Church *now,* Historic Tallmadge Church

115 Tallmadge Circle
Tallmadge, Ohio

National Register of Historic Places

David Bacon established Tallmadge in 1807 as a Congregational community. In 1821 local landowners donated timber to build the church, designed and constructed by one of Ohio's first architects, Lemuel Porter. The structure is considered to be an excellent example of New England style Federal architecture. The steeple is 100-feet high. The church was featured on the cover of Life Magazine in 1944, as an example of enduring American values. It is located on the town green of Tallmadge, an Akron suburb, and sits in the center of a busy traffic circle. The Ohio Historical Society has charge of the building, which is used for weddings and other special events as well as worship services.

Western Reserve College Chapel

115 College Street
Hudson, Ohio

Located on the Western Reserve Academy Campus.

Western Reserve College opened in 1826, the first institution of higher education in the Connecticut Western Reserve. The college was closely affiliated with the Presbyterian Church, for which it educated missionaries and ministers. In the 1820s and 1830s, the College became an important center of antislavery activity. Today the chapel is used for musical and other performances of the Western Reserve Academy.

1852 | GREEK REVIVAL | SUMMIT COUNTY

Baptist Church of Streetsboro
now,
Baptist Meetinghouse at Hale Farm and Village

2686 Oak Hill Road
Bath, Ohio

In 1833 thirteen settlers formed the Baptist Church in Streetsboro. The present church was built in 1852. Many church members were involved in the Civil War on the Union side. The building was slated for demolition in 1969, but was acquired by Hale Farm in 1970 and moved to its present location at the Village.

St. Mark's Episcopal Church

146 College Street
Wadsworth, Ohio

National Register of Historic Places

The church was built in 1841-42 by Congregationalist pioneers from New England who settled in the Western Reserve in 1814. The membership disbanded in 1885 and the building stood vacant for 7 years. It was purchased and restored by Pennsylvania German Mennonites in 1892. In 1959 the Mennonites built a new church and sold the building to the Episcopal Church, which had been meeting in a city recreation facility. The Episcopalians have extensively renovated the interior. The bell tower originally had a steeple, but this is now gone. The church is located on a small rise of land near the town square, and is the oldest structure in Wadsworth.

St. Martin of Tours Chapel

1800 Station Road
Valley City, Ohio

National Register of Historic Places

This parish was established in 1840, and founding members constructed a log church in 1841. The current chapel is the fourth for the parish, second on the site. All construction of the church was donated by local farmers, who gave a year of their time. "They did the plowing and then left the fields to the Lord's care. They dug clay and fired bricks within a short distance of the church. Legend says the harvest following was 'one of the best' in years." Completing and furnishing the interior of the church took 20 years, and includes Gothic altars and stations of the cross, pews and organ. In 1897, stained glass windows were installed. The steeple is 90 feet high with two bells. Located in the countryside outside of town, the church steeple is visible from surrounding farms. When the new church sanctuary was built in 2001, the old church became a chapel. *(www.stmartinvc.org)*

Zion Evangelical Lutheran Church

2233 Abbeyville Road
Valley City, Ohio

This congregation was established in 1831, and a wooden church was built at a nearby site in 1838. The church was founded by German settlers to Liverpool Township, and their services were exclusively in German until 1924. Men and women sat on opposite sides of the sanctuary. The present church is located in the countryside outside of Valley City, on a hillside adjacent to the church cemetery. Land for the church was donated by Mr. Coit, a Connecticut land developer. Church members dug the foundation and hauled block from a Berea quarry. The brick church has a 105-foot high tower with three bells.

Universalist Church

At the intersection of LeRoy and Greenwich Roads, on the town green Westfield Center, Ohio

This church is the oldest church in Medina County and the oldest Universalist Church in Ohio. The original congregation, some of whom came from the Connecticut Firelands, began meeting in local homes in 1821. Lumber and pews were donated by church members. In 1849, Abbie Danforth, a woman minister, was installed, in keeping with church practice of accepting both men and women as ministers. The church borders a large, well-maintained public green, along with other historic public buildings and private homes.

Immaculate Conception Church

708 Erie Street
Grafton, Ohio

National Register of Historic Places

The parish, originally in LaPorte, was organized in 1836-1840 as the first Catholic Church formed between Cleveland and Sandusky. In 1865 the church was moved to the present site in Grafton. The parish name was changed from St. John of the Cross to Immaculate Conception, and work began on a new building. Newly opened stone quarries brought German, Irish, and Polish workers to the area. The church was built to serve these immigrants, with stone mined from these same local quarries. During the 1890s the interior was frescoed and refurnished. The building has striking copper roofs on its three towers.

Christ Church Episcopal

162 South Main Street
Oberlin, Ohio

National Register of Historic Places

This parish was organized in 1855. The architect was Frank Wills. The church has notable stained glass windows, including one entitled "Courage" in the LaFarge tradition. The liturgy of the church has a tradition of musical and dramatic expression. The building is located on the main street, near the historic downtown.

First Church in Oberlin, United Church of Christ

106 North Main Street
Oberlin, Ohio

National Register of Historic Places

Congregationalists, mainly settlers from New England, organized the church in 1834. The congregation met in temporary settings until the current church was built in 1842. By 1860 it was among the largest Congregational churches in the country. Along with Berea, Tallmadge and other settlements in the Western Reserve, Oberlin was founded as a Congregationalist community. The church was part of the Underground Railroad and the meeting place of the Oberlin Anti-Slavery Society. The building is located adjacent to Oberlin College, which was founded by the congregation.

Columbia Baptist Church

25514 Royalton Road
Columbia Station, Ohio

National Register of Historic Places

Nineteen settlers formed the congregation in 1832. The first church on the site was built in 1840-48 and was torn down to make space for the current church. The church is located at the main intersection of the township, adjacent to the township hall, a cemetery, and another church. The sanctuary contains two beautiful stained glass windows. The Columbia Stone Quarry Co. donated the stone for the building, which church members carted in horse drawn farm wagons to the building site. Descendants remember stories of the many wagons broken while carrying the heavy loads of stone.

First United Methodist Church

127 Park Place
Wellington, Ohio

The congregation was organized in 1825-26. The inspiring steeple had a clock with four faces, one for each direction, and could be seen for miles. The steeple clock set the time for many people without clocks at home. The melodious bells that sounded the hour could be heard far out into the country and for years were used to sound fire alarms. The church borders a public green in the historic downtown, and is next to the Town Hall, which now houses the steeple clock. *(History of Lorain County)*

First Congregational United Church of Christ

140 South Main Street
Wellington, Ohio

The congregation, organized in 1824, first met in a log school house and built a brick church on the site in 1878-79. *History of Lorain County* relates that "During a winter revival meeting the church caught fire. As people started to stir, the preacher cried out 'Never mind the fire that water will quench, the fires of hell are what you need to fear.' However this had little effect and the congregation fled." The current church replaced the burned structure. Located downtown on the public green, it has exceptional stained glass windows and a dome in the sanctuary.

PUBLICATIONS OF THE CENTER FOR SACRED LANDMARKS
MAXINE GOODMAN LEVIN COLLEGE OF URBAN AFFAIRS,
CLEVELAND STATE UNIVERSITY

The Center for Sacred Landmarks is a research and public service center within the Maxine Goodman Levin College of Urban Affairs, Cleveland State University. The Center provides information about Cleveland's and northeast Ohio's religious structures and organizations and their past and present role in strengthening and maintaining communities within this region. The Center's four primary activities are researching and documenting the architectural and aesthetic features of religious structures; providing guidance or referrals to religious institutions that wish to preserve their archival materials and artworks, especially their stained glass windows; researching and documenting the human and social services engaged in by religious institutions; and researching and documenting the role that various religious institutions and their members have played in the history of the northeast Ohio region.

Religious institutions are repositories of invaluable historical information about the life of the community they serve. Unfortunately, many religious structures are at risk due to a combination of age and inadequate or deferred maintenance that has caused some to deteriorate. Records may be poorly maintained, or even destroyed by those unaware of their significance. In addition, changing demographic patterns may leave an institution with a congregation whose resources are not sufficient to maintain the building and/or its programs. The members of the Center for Sacred Landmarks at Cleveland State University hope that their research will provide a written and visual record of those structures that cannot be saved, and a foundation of information for those that can. The purpose of the Sacred Landmarks Publications Series is to provide a vehicle for the dissemination of this information highlighting the diversity and significance of the many religious communities in the northeast Ohio region, and beyond.

THE CENTER FOR SACRED LANDMARKS HAS THREE PUBLICATION SERIES.

THE MONOGRAPH SERIES features sacred art, architectural, and historical topics. Recent issues are richly illustrated and are published in full color in a 32 page, landscape format.

THE CATALOG SERIES represents collaboratively produced publications that accompany gallery exhibitions of sacred art and architecture. The format of these catalogs is similar to that of the Monograph Series.

THE PORTRAITS OF FAITH SERIES focuses on "snapshots" of whole groups of sacred landmarks of particular historical interest ("Village Churches") or current interest ("Megachurches"). Ideas presented in this series touch on topics such as economic development, sociology, and historical preservation. These publications are designed in a two color, portrait format.

The current publication is the inaugural issue of the *Portraits of Faith* series.

For more information on the Center for Sacred Landmarks and its publications, please consult the following Web site: http://urban.csuohio.edu/sacredlandmarks/

MICHAEL J. TEVESZ
Director, Center for Sacred Landmarks

ACKNOWLEDGEMENTS

Michael Tevesz, Ph.D. Director, Center for Sacred Landmarks

Douglas R. Hoffman, AIA, Series Editor, Principal with Weber Murphy Fox Architects

Chip Valleriano, Book design and layout

Norma Stefanik, Research Associate, Center for Urban and Regional Studies,
Youngstown State University

Beth Singer, Proofreading

The staff and volunteers of local historical societies and libraries in Ashtabula, Cuyahoga, Geauga, Lake, Lorain, Medina, Portage, and Trumbull Counties and the Western Reserve Historical Society.

Representatives and volunteers of the individual churches and denominations who generously provided information on their churches.

The organizations Preservation North Dakota and the State Historical Society of North Dakota, for their pioneering work on documenting prairie churches and their consultation with us.

The quotation from "Church Going" is from *The Less Deceived* by Philip Larkin and is reprinted by permission of The Marvell Press England and Australia.

Special thanks to the Rev. Richard T. Bennett and the congregation of Columbia Baptist Church, Lorain County, for permission to use the aerial photograph of the church, which is on the cover of this monograph. The State Aerial Farm Statistics Co. of Toledo, Ohio (www.stateaerial.com) took the photograph, and also kindly granted permission to reproduce it.

This work was done under contract to the Center for Public Administration and Public Policy, Kent State University. The authors and CPAPP gratefully acknowledge funding from the State of Ohio Urban University Program and the Northeast Ohio Research Consortium for supporting the research leading to this publication. This publication represents the ongoing collaboration between Cleveland State University and Kent State University as members of the Sacred Landmarks Partnership of Northeast Ohio. Funding for the design, printing, and publication of this work was provided by the Center for Sacred Landmarks, Cleveland State University.

While gratefully acknowledging the assistance provided by so many, we, the authors, are responsible for content, errors, and omissions.

REFERENCES

The Church of England, *The Church of England's Built Heritage*.
http://www.cofe.anglican.org/about/builtheritage/

Tarunjit Singh Butalia & Dianne P. Small, eds., *Religion in Ohio: Profiles of Faith Communities*. Ohio University Press, Athens, OH, 2004.

George W. Knepper, *A Brief History of Religion in Northeast Ohio*.
Center for Sacred Landmarks, Cleveland State University, Cleveland, OH, 2002.

Partners for Sacred Places, *America's Endangered Historic Urban Houses of Worship*.
Philadelphia, PA, no date. www.sacredplaces.org/

Philip Sheldrake, *Spaces for the Sacred: Place, Memory, and Identity*.
The John Hopkins University Press, Baltimore, MD, 2001.

E.V. Walter, *Placeways: A Theory of the Human Environment*.
The University of North Carolina Press, Chapel Hill, NC, 1988.

ISBN 0-9638675-7-1

© 2006 Cleveland State University